Indelible

Mary James Dansby

Dorrance Publishing Co
585 Alpha Drive
Pittsburgh, PA 15238
Visit our website at *www.dorrancebookstore.com*

ISBN: 979-8-88812-306-5
eISBN: 979-8-88812-806-0

⌒∿⌒

My desire for writing began over fifty years ago when the forced integration of public schools began. Terrified and confused, I was introduced to the world of English literature by an English teacher who made the works of Lord Byron, Wordsworth, and Poe come alive for me and are still alive in me today. My poems are a true reflection of my love for them. I have always said I would one day dedicate my poems to my children; however, the recent suicide of my 27-year-old niece exemplifies that they have always been for her. I have been published many times through the years in *Letters to the Editor* in *Abilene Reporter News*.

Gift of Love

A tear...
A flower...
A butterfly...
Life with its peaks and valleys
Until the day I die!

A cry...
A bird...
A bumblebee...
The endless search for immortality!

A laugh...
A peacock...
A dove...
So beautiful is this incessant gift of love!

Searching

My mind, heart, and soul is searching—
Throughout my country, world, and universe.
My very being reflects a need for love and nurturing.

To be touched by a child is to be touched by innocence—
Touched by purity, peace, and happiness.
To be touched by an angel is the beginning of repentance.

The questions that I need answered are about me—
I need to know the essence of everything.
To be loved and touched by God is pure piety.

Pure Perfection

To touch... to kiss... to embrace—
the physical aspects of my desire for you;
however, thinking of you always; feeling you
incessantly, and knowing that you love
me unconditionally is the reason why there
is a continuous rebirth of my soul.

An urge... a desire... intuitiveness—
the mental aspects of my wanting you; and
thinking of you, knowing that we are one
spiritually reflects the amazing truth of
our pure perfection together.

Ode to My God

Oh divine, almighty, gracious, majesty above;
Creator of all things—the greatest being love.
I sing to you with a soul so sweet and so pure;

 I sing of your goodness;

 I sing of your beauty;

 I sing of your magnificence;

And I sing of your mercy that you continuously procure!

Oh God... I see you in all that is wondrous and beautiful!

 I feel you in my soul which is spiritual and unsinful.

 I hear you in songs of peace, hope, and love;

 I taste you in all that is indelibly pious from above!

Homelessness

Under the bridge
Amongst strangers and rats
On a cold and windy night
In between hopelessness and despair
Near the brink of insanity.

With prayers to my God
In search of a response
Near cries of agony and defeat
Under utmost disbelief
Past hope of atonement.

Under the bridge
In the darkness of night
With hope of tomorrow
In search of my being
Without realizing the meaning of life.

Near the presence of my God
With all that delight
Under the most dire circumstances
During the search for life
In this overwhelming plight.

I Want To Live Forever

When I witness a falling star on a stary night,
My entire being shudders with pure delight;
I want to live forever!

When I hear raindrops falling gently on the roof,
My soul withdraws... it becomes aloof;
I want to live forever!

When I feel the overwhelming eeriness of the dark,
My entire being responds with a resounding remark;
I want to live forever!

When I lose to death ones that I truly love,
My soul cries out to my God above...
I want to live forever!

Love is Lost

Giving your heart and soul to someone you
Love—only to have them play with it
And give it back—creates a birth of
Overwhelming anger that holds your soul
Captive—the anger transcends the
Essence of your being—the agony holds
You captive forever—the love that
Was thought to be sweet and pure sours and
Is no more—love is lost!

The Game

I am magnificent, entertaining, and wild—
They play me with enthusiasm all the time.
A spectator is often seen acting like a child—
Shouting, swearing, and pumping fists as he whines.
All who know me love me as well—
Men, women, and children unite as one
To catch a glimpse of a legendary tale.
My hits are loud and too violent for some;
I am not for those who easily pale;
The power I possess will never be compromised.
The longer I exist, the more power I possess—
I am the obsession of men no matter their size.
"Full of sound and fury" and will be nothing less—
I am a God—I am FOOTBALL!

I Caught Life

I caught life in the palm of my hand—
I clenched my fist—I dared not let
It slip away; I feared I would not be
Able to capture it again.

Time passed—my fist grew weary—my
Grasp loosened; I frantically tried
To tighten my grip again; however, it was
To no avail—my hand opened—I cried out—
Life began to escape...

I anxiously attempted to close my hand; however,
I was too weak, too weary, too tired—I
Could not recapture it—life was lost...

From My Windows

From my windows, I see a world so remarkably true.
I see beautiful flowers covered with the morning's dew;
And as far as my eyes can see-
The marvels of nature overwhelm everything.

I see the sun as it breaks through the sky—
The undeviating and endless colors make me sigh;
For of all the wonders my eyes have ever beheld,
These amazing colors—above anything— will forever prevail.

I see birds in flight, chirping their songs—
Songs of love and peace—I have cherished for so long.
Their songs intensify as the sun shines brighter—
Making the burdens of this life seem so much lighter.

This beautiful day is conquering my mine—
Bringing peace, contentment, and spirituality so divine;
However, I see the sun suddenly began to set,
And beauty once again captures my heart in her glorious net!

Slowly darkness begins to cover everything—
Unfortunately, the creatures of the night began to sing.
I now know it is time to rest again
Until morning from my windows will once more begin.

Limitless

The many enlightening experiences that we are confronted with in life—the inability to sometimes understand or recall are remembered indelibly in the mind—even though a lack of knowledge regarding them exists—there are many expectations that are lost due to such frailties of the human spirit; thus, enhancing life to the fullest and spiriting life to death situations which sometimes may limit the growth of our souls and tailgate our existence while pleasure is perfected.

The logic and purity of the mind—the love and compassion of the heart—the fullness of our existence—the limitlessness of time—the vastness of space is what surpasses the rhythms of our most primitive urges; what we revel in may be pure, may be vile, but may be excitable to the many urges that engulf our souls.

To be what we are—to be who we want—to be all that we never were is to surpass the beginning of how we have become. Feeling pain— feeling agony— feeling peace—feeling love—reflects the overwhelming complexities of our total existence which coexists with what never was.

To Youth

Oh wayfaring youth;
It is time you watch out;
You are about to be rebuked;
Ole weary age is about.

Hear his footsteps as he slowly ascends your stairs;
Listen for his whip as he cracks it in the air;
He will be persistent with his knocks at your door;
He knows you will soon fade and be no more.

Overwhelmingly sad, because you can't run or hide;
Fulfilling prophecy, because his youth once died.
Ole weary age is coming—he comes with pride;
Fulfilling your destiny—you forgotten child.

My Mother Means The World To Me

My mother—she means the world to me;
She represents all that is wonderful and unique.
When I am hungry, she makes sure I am fed;
When I am ill, she tucks me gently in my bed.

Her touch seems to ease all my suffering and pain;
Her smile calms and most certainly entertains.
Her love makes life meaningful and clear,
Because God has given her wisdom—she keeps him near.

When she is sad, her tears fall gentle as the rain;
When death takes her—she will not complain.
Throughout eternity our bond will forever be;
May God bless her with everlasting peace,
Because my mother means the world to me.

Tears To My God

I look around—all around,
And I am overwhelmed with what I see.
I look up—I look down;
Life is strangling me!

I see forgotten men in cages made with chains;
I see weeping women being tormented and shamed.
I see sickness, misery, prejudice, and hate;
I cry tears to my God for the impending fate.

I look afar—I look near;
I observe this chaotic and evil situation.
I shudder and cry because of adulterated fear—
Lives are being lost in this powerful nation.

I see a weeping child all covered with dirt;
I see mothers agonizing—noticeably hurt.
I see filth, death, destruction—spoils of war;
Crying tears to my God, I once again look afar.

I Say

Socrates says, "Know thyself."
I say, "How can I less I find myself?'

Russians say, "Russia is not a nation, but a world."
I say, "America is not a world, but a universe!"

Karl Marx says, "Workers of the world unite."
I say, "Christians hold on to your faith!"

Some say, "God is dead!"
I say, "God help us all!"

Indelible

The pain in my soul is truly agonizing;
The indelible sorrow that engulfs my life overwhelms me.
The essence of truth and pure happiness is so tantalizing;
Yet, secrets of the unknown are what I seek.

TIME, LIFE, DEATH—they are truly infallible;
Protecting my soul is the epitome of my truth.
PAIN, SORROW, EUPHORIA—they are so indelible;
Furthermore, touching my soul as they erase my youth!

Advice From Momma

Advice from my momma is my truth and peace.
A beautiful and proud woman, she was indeed;
And the gift of encouragement she possessed;
Always instilled in me a desire to succeed.

She said, "There is nothing you can't achieve!
Be proud of yourself, and always find time for you.
Look for the good, and stay away from evil things;
After all, you can control what you feel and do!"

"Love our God and put him first;
Then, you know all will go perfectly well,
And one day when you are old and weary,
You will have a magnificent story to tell."

Always wear a smile on your beautiful face—
Even through life's ups and downs.
Don't ever disgrace who you are
By wearing a scowl or a frown!

You are God's special child;
Always remember this for me!
See the world for what it is,
And carry on my legacy!

My King

Though we have faced turmoil, stress, and frustration,
Our tumultuous love will solve this difficult equation.

Our relationship will one day set us free—
The trials and tribulations will enable us to see.

Our hearts have become one and simultaneously ring—
Sounding out to all that you are my beautiful king!

The Two

There was a tantalizing and mesmerizing aura to their walks—even from a distance. Dressed strikingly and superbly, they walked slowed towards each other with heads held high and shoulders proudly back. Each sported a pair of magnificent stilettos—one pair was gold and the other was silver.

Neither was beautiful—neither was comely; however, the boldness of their features made them appear extremely rugged and worn. There was something engaging about them as they approached each other. They were not speaking—the silence was deafening—the world appeared soundless at that moment.

At arm's length from each other, they still did not speak or nod—eyes piercing each other fiercely as they passed each other; however, the one who wore the gold stilettos turned around and asked in a loud, shrill voice, "Do I know you?" The other looked back, and with the voice that sounded like a trumpet, she replied, "I am Rona, and you?" The other laughed boldly, "I am Karma!"

This Plight

This plight—
A pestilence—silent, horrific, and overwhelming
Darkness allowed by God, despite...

This plight—
A pestilence—smothering, engulfing, and
Destroying—no respect for man's existence
Morning until night...

This plight—
A pestilence—plodding fiercely and unapologetically
While incessantly breeding fear and
Unadulterated fright...

This plight—
A pestilence—seeking love, seeking repentance,
Seeking God's forgiveness, despite...

Be Mine Forever

With you, life is really very beautiful;
Without you, it is ugly and gray;
So, I pray that you will be mine
Forever.

With you happiness is inevitable;
Without you it is never known;
So, I pray with all my heart that you will be mine
Forever.

With you my being revels in perfect pleasure;
Without you, it fades away;
So I pray with all my soul that you will be mine
Forever.

Most of All

To see you is to see perfection indeed.
Your features are stern;
Your features are exalting;
Your features are magnificent;
Most of all your features are mine to see.

To kiss you is to kiss and be set free.
Your kiss is firm;
Your kiss is warm;
Your kiss is tender;
Most of all your kiss is for me.

To touch you is to touch the smoothest tree.
You feel of strength;
You feel of stability;
You feel of sturdiness;
Most of all you feel of me.

To hear you is to hear a Sovereign King.
You speak with pride;
You speak with dignity;
You speak with authority;
Most of all you speak of me.

Two People in Love

When two people are in love,
They share the future and the past;
Living in the present,
They pray their love will last.

When two people are in love,
The problems of one are the problems of the other;
They share joy... they share sorrow;
Because they become one with each other.

When two people are in love,
Life seems sweet and full of array.
Lovers are joyous—they are peaceful,
Because love makes them that way.

When two people are in love,
They are a beautiful sight to behold—
They smile, they comfort, they caress,
For their love is more priceless than gold.

Time

Time! Time! Time! Please slow your trod down!
You are treading too fast without even making a sound!

It seems like only yesterday that we took our vows,
But many years have come and gone.
Your blade carves around my eyes, lips, and brows;
Your brother, DEATH, will soon snatch me from my home!

Old Man! Old Man! Hear my desperate plea;
Surely it is not too much what I ask of you...
Fling your cruel clocks into the roving sea...
Rest awhile, and have no more work to do.

Time! Time! Time! What has happened to my past?
You are treading—Old Man—much too fast!

Freedom

I walk... I walk... I walk... I happen upon a world—a world that frightens and perplexes me. I see a man all bound in chains—I see a broken woman lying in a pit of tears—I see a young boy in toil and agony—I see a young girl whose face is a mask of fear. I can see them clearly, and I hear them all as they cry out for FREEDOM.

I run... I run... I run... my mind races a million years—it feels as if it will explode! I think frantically to myself. What is this FREEDOM? Is it real? Can it be tasted, felt, or touched?

I am tired... so tired—I can run no further. I sit down to rest, and someone touches my shoulder. I look up into the face of an old woman who appeared old as time itself. She smiles at me; however, I can't smile back—fear has taken hold of me. I am trembling.

She wearily sits down beside me, and I ask in a trembling voice, "Who are you?" She does not answer me. Her eyes sparkling like diamonds, she only smiles. She looks away from me, but I know her eyes are searching me. Finally, she speaks; however, her mouth does not open. "Where are you running off to, Child?" I am now engulfed in my fear. I blurt out, "I am running to FREEDOM, ma'am!"

She laughs. Her laughter sounded like trumpets blaring. "To FREEDOM?" Her mouth still did not open.

"Yes mam-you know where it is?" My voice quivers.

She closes her eyes and speaks again without her mouth opening, "FREEDOM is in the heart—it is in your mind—it is in your soul—it is in a cool breeze that blows on a hot and blistery day—it is in a cup of cold water that soothes a parching tongue—it is overwhelming relief to the most tormenting pain—it is the manifested exaltation of euphoria!" She begins to cry, and her mouth remains closed.

My fear begins to subside... I feel compassion for her. I touch her arm as I look into her eyes, "Can I find it?"

She smiles at me again, "When you see the chains that bound men fall—when you see women smile with esteem—when you see boys playing in peace—when you see girls singing happily—when you can feel the presence of God; then, you know that you have found FREEDOM!"

I am confused. "If I don't find it, can I live without it?"

She does not smile. Her mouth opens for the first time! "To live without FREEDOM is to live without life... to live without it is to live without piety!" Her voice overpowers my ears. I shudder.

The old lady vanishes, and I am overtaken by fear again. I do not know where to look, but I know I must find FREEDOM! I walk... I walk... I walk...

Life

Life you are the greatest of multitudes of blessings;
You teach and enlighten me with priceless lessons.
You flood my existence with kisses so sweet—
Kisses that I yearn for and forever want to keep.
>Your kiss of light guides me each day;
>Your kiss of faith is my indelible ray;
>Your kiss of hope holds me in its grasp;
>Your kiss of wisdom interprets my past.

Life you are the bridge over my heart's ravine;
Your breath flows incessantly from my canteen.
Your magnificent juices also spew from it—
Juices that I desperately desire and must covet.
>Your juice of happiness tastes so divine;
>Your juice of peace is sweet and fine;
>Your juice of love tastes smooth and pure;
>Your juice of grace—God will procure.

Life... your antithesis, DEATH—he frightens me;
He will take you even though I will resist and plea.
He interrupts you with kisses that are blistery cold—
Kisses that are pungent, stagnant, and bold.
>His kiss of darkness is an insidious plight;
>His kiss of doom engulfs and destroys my sight.
>His kiss of despair tries to overpower my heart;
>And his kiss of destruction tears my identity apart.

Life... Death knows that his wrath is sure;
His horrible sting I will certainly endure;
His juices I despise and avoid tasting them when I can;
They only bring despair and misery to mortal man.

    His juice of sorrow has no taste;
    His juice of war fumes of pungent waste;
    His juice of hatred is bitter and incessant;
    And his juice of confusion is stale and malignant.

Life... the struggle is great between you and death;
He will soon overpower you and take away my breath.
He knows and boasts that his victory will be complete;
But I will meet you again in ETERNITY.

A Divided Nation

Everything exemplifies something! It is alarming and egregious how many circumstances that we are a part of reflect hypocrisy and contradictions. The very essence of our truths is lost in a spiraling parade of incessant facades.

How do we watch two humans pummel each other in a ring or cage? How do we take two years of a man's life for fighting dogs? How do we give a woman 20 years for shooting a gun into a wall? How do we acquit a man for stalking and murdering a boy for a lost cause?

Things that exemplify who we are, exemplify who we will become today and tomorrow. Tomorrow will find our empathy for each other lost among the stereotypes that we have inadvertently formed, and desires to be humane will be buried forever.

It is a travesty that there is a nation divided—a nation where all are caught up in alternate worlds that are on a collision course—society as we know it is wavering, and it may fall if caution is not taken to ensure peace and emphatically remind that the syllabus of our pledge has not become "with liberty and justice for dogs."

Lives That Matter Most

The unrest and hatred that plagues our nation is a reminder to all of us of man's purest imperfections. The futility of lives entwined in webs of deceit, confusion, and dismay reflect the totality of lost consciousness.

Does a rich man's life matter more than a poor man's? Does a white man's life matter more than a black man's? Truth be told—all lives matter equally, regardless of status or race; however, there is no finite answer to questions that for centuries have been loaded with ambiguities of tormented and lost souls.

Grasping at straws as we drown in our apathetic lives, a common ground needs to be reached to ensure that a search for respect for one another is the perfect goal to be realized; because the lives that matter most are the lives that epitomize the morals, grace, and values of our beautiful God.

The Murder of Innocence

The births of our beautiful children and the happiness of our beautiful children are the pinnacles of total exhilaration. The deaths of our precious children and the murders of our children epitomize the depths of agony and despair.

In our society, children lose their innocence and lives because of unrelenting and incessant sins due to overwhelming desires of an indulgent culture. Children lose their lives and are senselessly murdered because of presumptuous attitudes regarding rights rather than attention to wrongs—there is no regard for morals, values, or consequences.

The nakedness of our hearts—the nudeness of our souls—the immediate gratification of our desires has caused us to forget the innocence of a child, because we search recklessly and seem to need the very things that God despises. Our pursuit of immorality and egregious sins is a travesty—our spirituality has no power. We have discovered hell.

It is time to cry tears to our God. It is time to pray continuously in our homes, schools, and workplaces. It is time to ask God for wisdom, strength, and power to attain sacred goals.

I

I laugh;
I sing;
I rejoice;
I have all to give;
I'm overwhelmed—
I live!

I frown;
I cry;
I despair;
I can't find any purpose to live by;
I'm overwhelmed—I die.

www.ingramcontent.com/pod-product-compliance
Lightning Source LLC
Chambersburg PA
CBHW061647130726
47996CB00003B/1492